Clip-Art Features for Church Newsletters 3

Illustrations for Bulletin Boards,
Home Bulletins, and News Releases

Clip-Art Features for Church Newsletters 3

George W. Knight, Compiler
Howard Paris, Illustrator

BAKER BOOK HOUSE
Grand Rapids, Michigan 49506

Copyright 1987 by
Baker Book House Company

ISBN: 0-8010-5485-0

Fourth printing, March 1990

Printed in the United States of America

Contents

Introduction

1 Church Attendance and Support   9

2 Discipleship and Christian Growth   29

3 Evangelism and Witnessing   35

4 Family Life   49

5 Friendship and Interpersonal Relationships   61

6 Inspiration for Daily Living   77

7 Jesus Christ   105

8 Love   115

9 Prayer   121

10 Seasonal and Christian Year   129

Introduction

Churches are obviously searching for short fillers with visual appeal to publish in their newsletters and worship bulletins. The first two books of clip-art features, published by Baker Book House in 1984 and 1986, respectively, met with a good response. Howard Paris and I are delighted to respond to this continuing demand with *Clip-Art Features for Church Newsletters 3*.

Like the other two books in this series, this compilation of new material contains scores of copyright-free items, complete with copy, illustrations, and borders. To give your newsletter a special touch, just clip the features out of the book and paste them down on your newsletter layout sheet. They are ready-made for quality reproduction by copying machine, electronic stencil, or offset press.

We are glad to have a small part in your church's ministry through these practical books. Keep up the good work of publishing the Good News.

George W. Knight

1

Church Attendance and Support

Team Work

It's all very well to have courage and skill
    And it's fine to be counted a
    star,
But the single deed with its
touch of thrill
    Doesn't tell the man you
    are.

For there's no lone hand in the
game we play,
    We must work to a bigger
    scheme,
And the thing that counts in the
world today
    Is, How do you pull with the
    team?

They may sound your praise
and call you great,
    They may single you out for
    fame,
But you must work with your
running mate
    Or you'll never win the
    game.

Oh, never the work of life is
done
    By the man with a selfish
    dream,
For the battle is lost or the battle is won
    By the spirit of the team.
            —Edgar A. Guest

Comrades

Mr. Meant-To has a com-
rade,
    And his name is Didn't -
    Do;
Have you ever chanced to
meet them—
    Did they ever call on
    you?

These two fellows live together
    In the house of Never-
    Win,
And I'm told that it is
haunted
    By the ghost of Might-
    Have-Been.
            —Author unknown

A Definition of Faithfulness

God has a great ministry for our church. If we are to be effective, we must be involved in the ministry of our congregation. As you consider the question of faithfulness, answer the following questions:

1. If your car should start one out of three times, would you consider it faithful?
2. If your paperboy should skip your house on Sunday, would you call him faithful?
3. If you should fail to come to work two or three days a month, would your boss consider you faithful?
4. If your water heater should greet you with cold water one or two mornings a week, would it be faithful?
5. If you should miss a couple of house payments in a year, would your mortgage holder say that ten out of twelve wasn't too bad?

Thinking about these questions should give you a good idea of what faithfulness really is. Let's be faithful to God in our work through his church.

What If Our Church Should Close Its Doors?

If our church suddenly closed its doors, how long would it take people to discover we were no longer in business for the Lord?

Some would find out immediately, because they are often here for Bible study, worship, and fellowship. It would take others a few weeks to learn, because they do not attend services regularly. Still others would find out only when they needed the church for a wedding or a funeral. Lost people might pass by for months before realizing that nothing was happening at this place.

Who keeps the church open and alive? God, certainly. But never forget that God has chosen to work through his people. To the degree that we do not remain steadfast in our commitment to God, then to that same degree the work of God through his church is hindered.

Here's a sobering question for each of us to ask: If everyone treated the church exactly as I do, would it prosper or would it have to close its doors?

The Imperfect, Empowered Church

The New Testament tells about a church that had some real problems. But in spite of all these, it reached thousands of people for Christ.

This church was located in the wrong place. Most of the people in the community looked on the members of this church with scorn and ridicule. It didn't have a building in which to meet. Most of the members were on the verge of poverty.

The members of this church weren't trained for their jobs. Their membership was small—only about 120. The treasurer ran off with the church's money. What's more, the chief leader of this church had a way of putting his foot in his mouth. He was constantly making people angry.

To top it all off, there were divisions in this church. Several members were forced to flee to other cities because of persecution.

The one thing this church had going for it was the power of the Holy Spirit. It was the church in Jerusalem described in the Book of Acts. With all its problems, this church baptized 3,000 people after its first revival service.

What we need today are more imperfect churches empowered by the Holy Spirit.

How to Pull Together As a Church

Pull together in prayer: "Pray without ceasing" (1 Thess. 5:17). "And all things, whatsoever ye shall ask in prayer, believing, ye shall receive" (Matt. 21:22). Pray for each service of the church and the church staff.

Pull together in attendance: "Not forsaking the assembling of ourselves together . . ." (Heb. 10:25). Our faithful attendance will keep our church strong. It will also be a strong testimony for Christ to others in our community.

Pull together in giving: "Bring ye all the tithes into the storehouse . . ." (Mal. 3:10). The scriptural method of giving is the tithe. Give God what belongs to him. And do it in a generous, joyful spirit.

Every Church a Great Church

Beautiful is the large church,
  With stately arch and stee-
    ple;
Neighborly is the small church,
  With groups of friendly peo-
    ple.

Reverent is the old church,
  With centuries of grace;
And a wooden church or a
    stone church
  Can hold an altar place.

And whether it be a rich church
  Or a poor church anywhere,
Truly it is a great church
  If God is worshiped there.
                —Author unknown

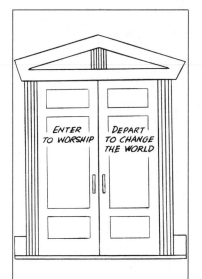

ENTER TO WORSHIP   DEPART TO CHANGE THE WORLD

The Church: A Redemptive Society

The church is never true to itself when it is living *for* itself, for if it is chiefly concerned with saving its own life, it will lose it. The nature of the church is such that it must always be engaged in finding new ways by which to transcend itself. Its main responsibility is always outside its own walls in the redemption of common life. That is why we call it a redemptive society.
                —Elton Trueblood

The Church
on the Avenue

God bless the church on the
  Avenue
  That hears the city's cry;
The church that sows the seed
  of the Word
  Where the masses of men
  go by.

A church that makes, in the
  traffic's roar,
  A place for an altar of prayer;
With a heart for the rich and a
  heart for the poor,
  And looks for the burden to
  share.

A church that is true to the call
  of the Christ
  Who wept for the city's need;
Who sent His disciples to labor for Him
  Where the forces of evil
  breed.

A church that gives and a
  church that lives
  As seen by the Master's
  eye;
God bless the church on the
  Avenue
  That answers the city's cry.
                    —Author unknown

Ten Ways to Build Up Your Church

1. Ignite the spiritual fires of your own soul.
2. Study your Bible with the aid of good resource materials.
3. Remember that people are the church; the place where you worship is a building.
4. Support your church with regular attendance.
5. Pray for your church's leaders.
6. Look for ways to encourage others in Christ.
7. Discover your unique way of witnessing to others, and do it often.
8. Give generously of your time, talents, money, and prayers.
9. Believe in your church and speak highly of its possibilities.
10. Invite people to attend church with you on Sunday.

Twelve Ways to Show Loyalty to Your Church

1. Fill your place; nobody else can.
2. Always do your best; sing, pray, and give.
3. Invite your neighbor to sing; two can praise God better than one.
4. Think holy things; your work will go more easily tomorrow.
5. Help the weak in faith; this is the command of Christ.
6. Find the discouraged; they need you.
7. Unite in every reasonable effort; you can make a difference.

8. Lift up the hands of your pastor; his helpfulness will be multiplied.
9. Next to you may be a stranger; find him.
10. Participate in every part of the service; you will get more out of it.
11. Sing in your soul as vigorously as with your lips; this is worship.
12. Smile; this will make others glad.

2

Discipleship and Christian Growth

Needed: Overlooking Christians

The church is made up of imperfect people. All of us have our faults. The amazing thing is that God has been able to work through imperfect Christians. He has never had an opportunity to work with any other kind.

The Christian who becomes preoccupied with criticizing others loses sight of the major cause. He gets wrapped up in details and misses the supreme design. His eyes wander from the crucified Christ to focus on the faults of those for whom Christ died. This causes his spiritual life to dry up.

What we need are Christians who overlook the faults of others as easily as they do their own.

My Influence

My life shall touch a dozen lives
　Before this day is done;
Leave countless marks for good or ill,
　Ere sets the evening sun.

So this the wish I always wish,
　The prayer I ever pray—
"Lord, may my life help other lives
　It touches by the way."
　　　　　—Author unknown

The Real Question

It's not what you'd do with a
    million
If riches should e'er be
    your lot,
But what are you doing at
    present
With the ten-dollar bill
    you've got?
    —Author unknown

WORK · GIVE · PRAY · WORK · GIVE · PRAY

Steps of Christian Growth

Pray without ceasing (1 Thess. 5:17).
Rejoice in the Lord alway (Phil. 4:4).
Add to your faith virtue (2 Peter 1:5).
Ye have not, because ye ask not (James 4:2).

Whatsoever he saith unto you, do it (John 2:5).
Only fear the LORD, and serve him (1 Sam. 12:24).
Remember the words of the Lord Jesus (Acts 20:35).
Keep thyself pure (1 Tim. 5:22).

Go ye into all the world, and preach (Mark 16:15).
In all thy ways acknowledge him (Prov. 3:6).
Vow, and pay unto the LORD (Ps. 76:11).
Endure hardness, as a good soldier of Jesus Christ
                                    (2 Tim. 2:3).

GIVE · PRAY · WORK · GIVE · PRAY · WORK · GIVE

3

Evangelism and Witnessing

Portrait of a Prospect

Prospects aren't strange creatures whom someone else finds and reports to the church. Prospects are real live people whom you meet every day. The supermarket clerk, the beautician, the bank teller, the school teacher, your next-door neighbor or friend—all these may be people whom our church should reach with the gospel.

A prospect is a person who needs Jesus Christ as Savior. This includes everyone within the range of your witness who is not a Christian. Another type of prospect is a Christian who has moved to your community and needs a church home.

Do you know a prospect? Witness to him. Try to reach him for Jesus Christ and the church.

Fruitful Visit

One day I rang a doorbell
  In a casual sort of way;
'Twas not a formal visit
  And there wasn't much to say.

I don't remember what I said—
  It matters not, I guess—
But I found a heart in hunger,
  A soul in deep distress.

He said I came from heaven,
  And I've often wondered why;
He said I came to see him
  When no other help was nigh.

It meant so little to me
  To knock at a stranger's door,
But it meant heaven to him
  And God's peace forevermore.
    —Author unknown

Witnessing to a Neighbor

Sharing Christ with others is a privilege as well as a responsibility. Here are some practical "bridges" that can help you to share Christ with your neighbor.

1. Find out when his birthday is and send him a card with a friendly note.
2. Offer to cut his grass and take his mail in when he goes away on vacation.
3. Take him some homemade bread, cookies, and so on.
4. Invite him over to your house for a cookout or picnic.
5. Smile at him whenever you see him. You'll be surprised how this helps after a hard day's work!
6. If he is a new neighbor, a little "housewarming" gift can really minister to him and express your thoughtfulness.
7. If he has little children, offer to babysit for him at times.
8. If he should be admitted to the hospital, visit him and offer to take care of things at home.

In witnessing to a neighbor, you'll find that a little thoughtfulness goes a long way.

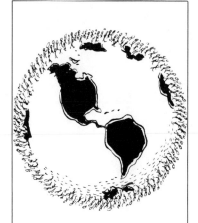

The Urgency of Witnessing

Here are some shocking statistics that emphasize the urgency of witnessing for Christ:

1. When you arrive at your Sunday school class next week, there will be 1,000,000 more lost people in the world than when you arrived last Sunday.
2. About 200,000 people will die around the world within the next twenty-four hours. Most of them will not know Christ as Savior and Lord.
3. A line made up of all the lost people in the world would circle the earth thirty times. This line grows at the rate of twenty miles per day.

Keep On Going

One step won't take you
very far;
    You've got to keep on
    walking.
One word won't tell people
who you are;
    You've got to keep on
    talking.

One inch won't make you
very tall;
    You've got to keep on
    growing.
One little call won't do it all;
    You've got to keep on
    going.

A New Resident Is Waiting for Your Visit

He has just moved into town. He will need a church home. He and his family also need Christian fellowship and spiritual training.

He needs to know about our church program as well. He may have children who should be enrolled in Sunday school.

He may be very lonesome with no friends in a strange neighborhood. His wife may need a friend to show her around town. He has questions about enrolling the children in school. He needs a place to worship this Sunday.

He's waiting for your visit. Are *you* on your way?

An Invitation Makes a Difference

On Monday a friend met me on the street. "I noticed you were absent from our last civic club meeting," he said. "Will you be there next Wednesday?"

"No," I replied. "I can't make it. Don't look for me."

Two men asked me on Tuesday if I could come. I said to the first, "I wish I could, but I can't this week." The next one I told, "My schedule looks impossible, but I'll try to find the time to come."

Wednesday morning in the post office a fourth man asked if I would be at the meeting that day. "I'll try to come," I replied, "but I may not make it." Before I got to my car, a fifth man stopped me, and I promised I would be there for sure.

I don't know whose official duty it was to contact me, but I couldn't resist the invitation from five different men. We all like to go where we are wanted. If you want the unsaved, the indifferent, and absentees to attend church, you must let them know. If you really want them to come, you will find the opportunity to invite them. This is a task for every member of our church.

What Outreach and Witnessing Will Do for a Church

Outreach and Christian witnessing will do several good things for a church:

It will kill bickering, criticism, and complaining. People who are busy witnessing for Christ don't have time for such trivial things.

It will revive the church. A church can witness for Christ only in the spirit of consecration and prayer. When these graces are practiced, the things which displease the Lord will be removed.

It will encourage unaffiliated church members to move their membership. For every person who makes a profession of faith during a worship service, usually two others will transfer their membership to the church.

It will kindle a kindred spirit in other church members. When we notice a fellow church member witnessing for Christ, we ask, "Why can't I do that?"

True greatness is possible for a congregation when it becomes a witnessing and winning church.

4

Family Life

The Miracle of Birth

Of all the wondrous miracles
  That happen on this earth,
I think the one that thrills me
    most
  Is the miracle of birth.

As I look down at your little
    face,
  At your tiny feet and hands,
My heart is filled with love for
    you
  And my head is filled with
    plans.

Plans for holding you close to
    me
  And plans for games and
    fun,
The blessings of watching you
    as you learn
  To talk and walk and run.

So I welcome you into this
    world
  With a thankful prayer of
    love,
For you, my precious baby,
  Are a gift from God above.
              —Pattie York

Before It Is Too Late

If you have a tender mes-
    sage
  Or a loving word to say,
Do not wait till you forget it,
  But whisper it today;
The tender word unspoken,
  The letter never sent,
The long forgotten mes-
    sages,
  The wealth of love un-
    spent—
For these some hearts are
    breaking,
  For these some loved
    ones wait;
So show them that you care
    for them
  Before it is too late.
              —Frank Herbert Sweet

A Little Fellow Follows Me

A careful man I ought to be,
A little fellow follows me;
I do not dare to go astray
For fear he'll go the selfsame
way.

Not once can I escape his
eyes;
Whate'er he sees me do, he
tries.
Like me he says he's going to
be
That little chap who follows
me.

He thinks that I am good and
fine;
Believes in every word of
mine.
The base in me he must not
see—
That little chap who follows
me.

I must remember as I go
Thru summer sun and winter
snow,
I'm building for the years to be
For that little chap who follows
me.

—Author unknown

The Heart of a Child

Whatever you write on the
heart of a child
No water can wash away;
The sand may be shifted
when billows are wild
And the efforts of time
may decay.

Some stories may perish,
Some songs be forgot,
But this graven record—
Time changes it not.

Whatever you write on the
heart of a child,
A story of gladness or
care,
That heaven has blessed or
earth has defiled,
Will linger unchangeable
there.

—Author unknown

Beatitudes for Parents

Blessed are parents who make their peace with mud and spilled milk, for of such is the kingdom of childhood.

Blessed are parents who refuse to compare their children with others, for each is precious.

Blessed are fathers and mothers who have learned to laugh, for it is the music of the child's world.

Blessed are parents who can say no without anger, for comforting to the child is the security of a firm decision.

Blessed are parents who accept the awkwardness of their growing children, letting each grow at his own speed.

Blessed are parents who are teachable, because knowledge brings understanding and love.

Blessed are parents who love their children in the midst of a hostile world, for love is the greatest of all gifts.

A Father's Prayer

Give me a son, O Lord, who will be strong enough to know when he is weak, and brave enough to face himself when he is afraid—one who will be proud and unbending in honest defeat, and humble and gentle in victory.

Give me a son whose wishes will not take the place of deeds; a son who will know thee—and that to know himself is the foundation stone of true knowledge.

Lead him, I pray, not in the path of ease and comfort, but under the stress and strains of difficulties and challenges, let him learn to stand up in the storm. Let him also learn compassion for those who fail.

Give me a son whose heart will be clear, whose goal will be high—a son who will master himself before he seeks to master others—one who will reach into the future, yet never forget the past.

And after all these things, add enough of a sense of humor so he may always be serious, yet never take himself too seriously. Give him humility so he may always remember the simplicity of true wisdom and the meekness of true strength.

—Douglas MacArthur

The Sin of Indifference

What word is the opposite of *love*? Most of us would say *hate.* But hate is not the opposite of love. The opposite of love is indifference.

When a husband or wife says "I hate you," the case is not hopeless. That marriage can be saved. But when a husband or wife becomes totally indifferent to the other, that marriage is in real jeopardy.

Nothing hurts our Lord more than indifference. He prefers being hated to being ignored. I wonder how Jesus feels about those who are indifferent and apathetic toward their church?

5

Friendship and Interpersonal Relationships

Locked In

She built herself a little
house
  All walled around with
  Pride;
Took Prudence as a servant
  And locked herself in-
  side.

She drew the blinds down
tight as tight
  When Sorrow chanced
  to roam;
Experience called—she
sent out word
  That she was not at
  home.

Then wherefore should she
now complain
  And wherefore should
  she sigh,
That Life and Love and
Laughter
  Have passed, unseeing,
  by?
          —Author unknown

Erasers of the Heart

Erasers are the nicest
things!
  Of that there is no doubt;
We write wrong words—a
few quick swipes
  And big mistakes fade
  out.

And you will find erasers
  Of a very different kind
Extremely helpful if you will
try
  To bear these facts in
  mind:

When you bump someone
in a crowd
  And almost knock him
  down,
A soft "I'm sorry" may bring
smiles
  And rub out that old
  frown.

Apologies, invariably,
  Obliterate mistakes;
And three small words, "I
love you!"
  Can erase the worst
  heartaches.
          —Author unknown

The Magic of a Laugh

A laugh is just like sun-
    shine—
    It freshens all the day,
It tips the peak of life with
    light
    And drives the clouds
    away.

The soul grows glad that
    hears it
    And feels its courage
    strong;
A laugh is just like sunshine
    For cheering folks along.

A laugh is just like music;
    It lingers in the heart,
And where its melody is
    heard
    The ills of life depart.

And happy thoughts come
    crowding
    Its joyful notes to greet:
A laugh is just like music
    For making living sweet.
        —Author unknown

Outwitted

He drew a circle that shut
    me out—
Heretic, rebel, a thing to
    flout;
But Love and I had the wit to
    win:
We drew a circle that took
    him in!
        —Edward Markham

What to Forget and Remember

Forget each kindness that you do
  As soon as you have done it;
Forget the praise that falls to you
  The moment you have won it;
Forget the slanders that you hear
  Before you can repeat it;
Forget each slight, each spite,
  each sneer,
    Wherever you may meet it.

Remember every kindness done
  To you whate'er its measure;
Remember praise by others won
  And pass it on with pleasure;
Remember every promise made
  And keep it to the letter;
Remember those who lend you aid,
  And be a grateful debtor.

Remember all the happiness
  That comes your way in living;
Forget each worry and distress,
  Be hopeful and forgiving;
Remember good, remember truth,
  Remember heaven's above you;
And you will find through age and youth
  True joys, and hearts to love you.

—Priscilla Leonard

Destructive Anger

When I have lost my tem-
    per,
  I have lost my reason too;
I'm never proud of anything
  Which angrily I do.

When I have talked in anger
  And my cheeks are flam-
    ing red,
I have always uttered
    something
  That I wish I hadn't said.

In anger I have never done
  A kindly deed, or wise;
But many things for which I
    know
  I should apologize.

In looking back across my
    life
  And all I've lost or made,
I can't recall a single time
  When anger ever paid.
          —Author unknown

Too Late

Strange that I did not know
    him then,
  That friend of mine.
I did not even show him
    then
  One friendly sign,

But cursed him for the ways
    he had
  To make me see
My envy of the praise he
    had
  For praising me.

I would have rid the earth of
    him
  Once, in my pride.
I never knew the worth of
    him
  Until he died.
          —Edwin Arlington
            Robinson

69

Eight Tips for Creative Living

1. Learn to laugh; a hearty laugh is much better than medicine.
2. Learn to mind your own business; few people can handle their own well.
3. Learn to tell a story; a well-told story is like a sunbeam in a sickroom.
4. Learn to say kind things; nobody ever resents them.
5. Learn to stop grumbling; if you can't see any good in the world, at least keep the bad to yourself.
6. Learn to love other people; this is a doorway to the kingdom.
7. Learn to put yourself in the other person's place before condemning; it might change your outlook.
8. Learn the lessons of the Bible; no greater ones are available to guide our daily lives.

A Friend Or Two

You do not need a score of
men to laugh and sing
with you;
You can be rich in com-
radeship with just a friend
or two.
You do not need a monarch's
smile to light your way
along;
Through good or bad a friend
or two will fill your days
with song.

When winds of failure start to
blow, you'll find the throng
has gone—
The splendor of a brighter
flame will always lure
them on;
But with the ashes of your
dreams, and all you
hoped to do,
You'll find that all you really
need is just a friend or
two.

So let the throng go on its way
and let the crowd depart;
But one or two will keep the
faith when you are sick at
heart;
And rich you'll be, and com-
forted, when gray skies
hide the blue
If you can turn and share your
grief with just a friend or
two.

               —Author unknown

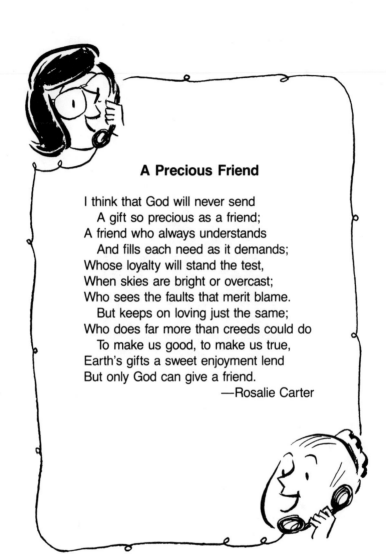

A Precious Friend

I think that God will never send
   A gift so precious as a friend;
A friend who always understands
   And fills each need as it demands;
Whose loyalty will stand the test,
When skies are bright or overcast;
Who sees the faults that merit blame.
   But keeps on loving just the same;
Who does far more than creeds could do
   To make us good, to make us true,
Earth's gifts a sweet enjoyment lend
But only God can give a friend.

              —Rosalie Carter

6

Inspiration for Daily Living

Thinking Positive Thoughts

Think of the things that make you
happy,
  Not the things that make you
  sad;
Think of the fine and true in man-
kind,
  Not its sordid side and bad;
Think of the blessings that sur-
round you,
  Not the ones that are denied;
Think of the virtues of your friend-
ships,
  Not the weak and faulty side.

Think of the gains you've made in
business,
  Not the losses you've incurred;
Think of the good of you that's
spoken,

Not some cruel, hostile word;
Think of the days of health and
pleasure,
  Not the days of woe and pain;
Think of the days alive with sun-
shine,
  Not the dismal days of rain.

Think of the hopes that lie before
you,
  Not the waste that lies behind;
Think of the treasures you have
gathered,
  Not the ones you've failed to
  find;
Think of the service you may ren-
der,
  Not of serving self alone;
Think of the happiness of others,
  And in this you'll find your own!
                              —Robert E. Farley

The Person I'd Like to Be

People are of two kinds,
    and he
Was the kind I'd like to be.
Some preach their virtues,
    and a few
Express their lives by what
    they do;
That sort was he. No flow-
    ery phrase
Or glibly spoken word of
    praise
Won friends for him. He
    wasn't cheap
Or shallow, but his course
    ran deep,
And it was pure. You know
    the kind.
Not many in life you find
Whose deeds outrun their
    words so far
That more than what they
    seem, they are.
            —Author unknown

Prescription for Loneliness

Art thou lonely, O my
    brother?
Share thy little with another!
Stretch a hand to one un-
    friended,
And thy loneliness is ended.
            —John Oxenham

Growing Old

Let me grow lovely, growing
    old—
    So many fine things do—
Laces, and ivory, and gold,
    And silks need not be
    new;
And there is healing in old
    trees,
    Old streets a glamour
    hold;
Why may not I, as well as
    these,
    Grow lovely, growing old?
            —Karle Wilson Baker

Time

So the sands of Time that
    slowly flow
From out my hour glass
Will all too soon have ebbed
    away;
    My life will then be past.

So I must make the most of
    time
And drift not with the tide;
For killing time's not
    murder—
It's more like suicide.
        —Author unknown

We Have Today

Today is ours—let's live it.
And love is strong—let's
    give it.
A song can help—let's sing
    it.
And peace is dear—let's
    bring it.

The past is gone—don't
    fret it.
Our work is here—let's do
    it.
The world is wrong—let's
    right it.
If evil comes, let's fight it.

The road is rough—let's
    clear it.
The future vast—don't fear
    it.
Is faith asleep—let's wake
    it.
Today is free—let's take it.
        —Lydia L. Roberts

Insights from Flying Geese

Perhaps you have seen geese flying through the sky in a "V" formation. Christians can learn some valuable lessons from their habits.

Flying in a "V" formation decreases the wind drag for all but the lead goose. The uplift of the wings of the bird in front make it easier for the flock to fly long distances. Christians can learn from this that we always accomplish far more by working together than by acting individually. That's why God created the church and instructed us to "bear one another's burdens." When we share a common goal and work together in harmony, there is no limit to what can be accomplished.

When flying together in a "V," the lead goose will drop back into the formation to rest a bit while another takes his place as the leader. We can learn from this that it pays to take turns doing the hard jobs, lest a few become "weary in well doing." What excuses have you been giving God when asked to serve?

Seasoned goose observers have also noticed that when a goose becomes ill or wounded and falls out of formation, two others will fall out with him and remain behind to nurse him until he recovers enough to join another flock. What a lesson we Christians can learn from this!

Why do we condemn those of our number who fall rather than love and nurse them back to wholeness? If the world knew we would love unconditionally and stand by one another no matter what, we would have to build thousands of new churches to accommodate all the people.

God's Will and How to Find It

How do you find God's will in specific situations? Henry Drummond suggests taking these eight actions:

1. Pray.
2. Think.
3. Ask wise people for their counsel, but don't let them tell you exactly what you should do.
4. Beware of the bias of your own will, but don't be too afraid of it. God doesn't necessarily thwart a person's desire. God's will and what you would like to do may be one and the same.
5. Meanwhile, do the next logical thing that must be done. Doing God's will in small things is the best preparation for finding it in great things.
6. When the time of decision comes, act on the knowledge you have.
7. Never reconsider the decision, once you have acted on it.
8. Be patient. You may not discover until long afterward that God was leading every step of the way.

Taking Life Seriously

To realize how short life really is, think of a life span of seventy years as a single day—from 7:00 in the morning until 11:00 at night. If your age is:

15, the time is 10:25 A.M.
20, the time is 11:34 A.M.
25, the time is 12:42 P.M.
30, the time is 1:51 P.M.
35, the time is 3:00 P.M.
40, the time is 4:08 P.M.
45, the time is 5:16 P.M.
50, the time is 6:25 P.M.
55, the time is 7:34 P.M.
60, the time is 8:42 P.M.
65, the time is 9:51 P.M.
70, the time is 11:00 P.M.

This exercise reminds us that we don't have a lot of time to serve God. Let's get busy and make every day count for him.

Sorrow's Lessons

I walked a mile with Plea-
sure!
She chattered all the way,
But left me none the wiser
For all she had to say.

I walked a mile with Sorrow
And ne'er a word said
she;
But oh, the things I learned
from her
When Sorrow walked
with me!
—Robert Browning
Hamilton

Ten Routes to Misery

If your goal is to be misera-
ble most of the time, here are
ten actions that will help you
reach this state in record time.

1. Think and talk about yourself; drop "I" into every
   conversation.
2. Expect to be appreciated.
3. Pay close attention to
   what people say about
   you.
4. Cultivate suspicion, jeal-
   ousy, and envy.
5. Be sensitive to slights and
   never forgive a criticism.
6. Trust nobody but yourself.
7. Demand that everyone
   agree with your views on
   every issue.
8. Insist on being given special consideration.
9. Don't take your duties and
   responsibilities seriously.
10. Do as little as possible for
    other people.

On the other hand, if you
want to be happy, do just the
opposite of these ten actions.
This will turn misery into joy!

A Definition of Character

Character is like a tree and reputation is like its shadow. The shadow is what we think of it; the tree is the real thing.

—Abraham Lincoln

A Quality of Mind

Age is a quality of mind—
If you've left your dreams behind;
If hope is cold;
If you no longer look ahead;
If your ambitious fires are dead—
Then you are old!

—Author unknown

No Fear

Though my soul may set in darkness,
It will rise in perfect light;
I have loved the stars too fondly
To be fearful of the night.

—Author unknown

Yesterday's Worries

Take yesterday's worries and sort them all out
And you'll wonder whatever you worried about;
Look back at the cares that once furrowed your brow—
I fancy you'll smile at most of them now.
They seemed terrible then, but they really were not;
For once out of the woods, all the fears are forgot.
—Author unknown

Friendly Obstacles

For every hill I've had to climb,
   For every stone that bruised
      my feet,
For all the blood and sweat
      and grime,
   For blinding storms and
      burning heat,
My heart sings but a grateful
      song—
These were the things that
      made me strong.

For all the heartaches and the
      tears,
   For all the anguish and the
      pain,
For gloomy days and fruitless
      years,
   And for the hopes that lived
      in vain,
I do give thanks, for now I
      know
These were the things that
      helped me grow!

'Tis not the softer things of life
   Which stimulate man's will
      to strive;
But bleak adversity and strife
   Do most to keep our will
      alive.
O'er rose-strewn paths the
      weaklings creep,
But brave hearts dare to climb
      the steep.
                    —Author unknown

Measuring the Load

It's easy to sit in the sun-
      shine
   And talk to the man in the
      shade;
It's easy to sit in a well-
      made boat
   And tell others where to
      wade.

It's easy to tell the toiler
   How best to carry his
      pack;
But you'll never know the
      weight of the load
   Till the pack is on your
      back!
                    —Author unknown

Strength for the Asking

A little boy was having a hard time lifting a heavy stone. His father asked, "Are you using all your strength?"

"Yes, I am," the boy replied.

"No you're not," said the father. "I'm right here waiting, and you haven't asked me to help."

When we are faced with a problem that seems unsolvable or a burden that is too heavy, we might ask ourselves, "Are we using all our strength?" Our Father, too, is waiting to help.

A Living Sermon

I'd rather see a sermon
    Than hear one any day;
I'd rather one should walk
    with me
    Than merely tell the way.

The eye's a better pupil
    And more willing than the
    ear;
Fine counsel is confusing,
    But example's always
    clear.

And the best of all the
    preachers
    Are the men who live
    their creeds;
For to see good put in action
    Is what everybody
    needs.
        —Edgar A. Guest

97

Cheering the Winners

If I should win, let it be by the code
  With my faith and my honor held high;
But if I should lose, let me stand by the road
  And cheer as the winners go by.
                        —Author unknown

God of the Commonplace

If God is not in your typewriter as well as your hymnbook, there is something wrong with your religion. If God does not enter your kitchen, there is something wrong with your kitchen. If you can't take God into your recreation, there is something wrong with your play.

We all believe in the God of the heroic. What we need most is the God of the humdrum—the commonplace, the everyday.

—Peter Marshall

The Things We Need

Some things a man must
surely know,
If he is going to live and grow:
He needs to know that life is
more
Than what a person lays in
store;
That more than all he may ob-
tain,
Contentment offers greater
gain.

He needs to feel the thrill of
mirth,
To sense the beauty of the
earth,
To know the joy that kindness
brings
And all the worth of little
things;
He needs to have an open
mind,
A friendly heart for all man-
kind.

A trust in self—without con-
ceit—
And strength to rise above de-
feat;
He needs to have the will to
share,
A mind to dream, a soul to
dare,
A purpose firm, a path to plod,
A faith in man, a trust in God.
—Alfred Grant Walton

Things Worthwhile

These things make life
worthwhile to me:
A sunset sky, a maple tree;
A mountain standing grim
and gray
Against the skyline far
away;
A baby's laugh, a summer
breeze,
A roadway winding 'neath
the trees;
A friend to trust, a book to
read,
And work which meets
some human need;
And through it all, a sense
of God
Lifting my soul above the
sod;
The hope and peace which
He can give—
These make it worth my
while to live.
—Author unknown

7

Jesus Christ

Our Riches in Christ

In Christ we have:

- A love that can never be fathomed.
- A life that can never die.
- A peace that can never be understood.
- A rest that can never be disturbed.
- A joy that can never be diminished.
- A hope that can never be disappointed.
- A glory that can never be clouded.
- A happiness that can never be interrupted.
- A light that can never be extinguished,
- A strength that can never be overcome.
- A beauty that can never be marred.
- A purity that can novor bo defiled.
- Resources that can never be exhausted.

Count on Jesus

If wind or wave should sweep away
  Those things I now hold dear;
If health should flee and sickness come,
  Or loved ones leave me here.

Should fortunes change and hardship come,
  If dreams should fade away;
If tests and trials should plague me sore,
  And troubles haunt my day.

When all is gone, this still I know,
  Christ's love will never leave us,
For when all things have passed away,
  We still can count on Jesus.
    —Author unknown

Jesus My All

Christ my Savior, Christ my
friend,
Christ my treasure without end;
Christ when waves of sorrow roll,
Christ the comfort of my soul.
Christ when all around should fail,
Christ when enemies prevail;
Christ when false accusers rise,
Christ my solace in the skies.

Christ when days are dark and
drear,
Christ when all around is clear;
Christ when all the earth is gone,
Christ my portion on the throne.

Christ at home and Christ abroad,
Christ my company on the road;
Christ in sickness, Christ in
health,
Christ in poverty and wealth.

Christ who once on earth has
trod,
Christ the blessed Son of God;
Christ for now and Christ for then,
Christ my Savior and my friend.
—Author unknown

The Sufficient Christ

I need a strength to keep
    me true
And straight in everything I
    do;
I need power to keep me
    strong
When I am tempted to do
    wrong.

I need a grace to keep me
    pure
When passion tries its
    deadly lure;
I need a love to keep me
    sweet
When hardness and mis-
    trust I meet.

I need an arm to be my stay
When dark with trouble
    grows my day:
And naught on earth can
    these afford,
But all is found in Christ my
    Lord.
                —Theodore Horton

Jesus Understands

I sat upon the edge one day
  To cast my gaze below,
Observing what was said and
    done
  By men I did not know.

Thus caught my eye a horrid sight
  I all but understood;
And jumping up, my head amiss,
  Flew quickly as I would.

Before my King I humbly came,
  Cast on my knees in praise;
With quiet voice and aching heart
  I questioned all man's ways.
He picked me up with gentle
    hands
  And searched me with His
    eyes;
He set me there before His throne
  And turned to part the skies.

He told me then of man He loved,
  Who breathed His very breath;
He told me how He gave them all,
  By suffering, in His death.

"And yet," cried I, "they love you
    not,
  But few do seek your name;
There seems no thought of
    heaven or hell;
  For them life's just a game."

He turned His head—I saw the
    tears—
  As He watched the world be-
    low;
Then breathed to me a painful
    sigh,
  "I know, my child, I know."

—David J. Heyen

8

Love

Where Love Abides

I turned an ancient poet's
    book
  And found upon the
    page,
"Stone walls do not a prison
    make
  Or iron bars a cage."

Yes, that is true, and some-
    thing more
  You will find where'er you
    roam
That marble floors and
    gilded walls
  Can never make a home.

But everywhere that love
    abides
  And friendship is a guest
Is surely home, and home
    sweet home—
  For there the soul can
    rest.
            —Henry Van Dyke

The Many
Expressions of Love

Love is silence—when your
    words would hurt;
Love is patience—when
    your neighbor is curt.
Love is deafness—when a
    scandal flows;
Love is thoughtfulness—
    for others' woes.
Love is promptness—
    when stern duty calls;
Love is courage—when
    misfortune falls.
        —Author unknown

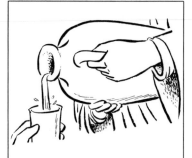

What Is Love?

Love is an attitude—love is
a prayer,
For a soul in sorrow, a heart
in despair;
Love is good wishes for the
gain of another,
Love suffers long with the
fault of a brother.

Love giveth water to a cup
that's run dry;
Love reaches low, as it can
reach high;
Seeks not her own at ex-
pense of another;
Love reaches God when it
reaches our brother.
—Author unknown

9

Prayer

You Prayed for Me

You did not know my need,
Or that my heart was sore
  indeed,
Or that my fears I could not
  quell,
But you sensed that some-
  thing wasn't well,
  And so you prayed for
  me.

My path had turned from
  light to black,
There seemed to be no
  turning back,
Then in my loneliness I felt
  God near,
And down the road a light
  dawned clear
  Because you prayed for
  me.

And as your prayer to
  heaven soared,
God did on me a blessing
  pour—
  The day you prayed for
  me.
  —Author unknown

The Simplicity of Prayer

Prayer is so simple,
It is like quietly opening the
  door
And slipping into the very
  presence of God;
There in the stillness
To listen to His voice;
Perhaps to petition
Or only to listen.
It matters not;
Just to be there in His pres-
  ence
Is prayer.
  —Author unknown

The Story of the Praying Hands

For years people have admired the art masterpiece known as "The Praying Hands." Behind this work of art is a fascinating story of love and sacrifice.

In the late fifteenth century two struggling young art students, Albrecht Dürer and Franz Knigstein, worked as laborers to earn money for their art studies. But the work was long and hard and it left them little time to study art.

Finally they agreed to draw lots and let the loser support them both while the winner continued to study. Albrecht won, but he agreed to support Franz after achieving success so his friend could finish his studies.

After becoming successful, Albrecht sought out Franz to keep his bargain. But he soon discovered the enormous sacrifice his friend had made. As Franz had worked at hard labor, his fingers had become twisted and stiff. His long, slender fingers and sensitive hands had been ruined for life. He could no longer manage the delicate brush strokes so necessary for executing fine paintings. But in spite of the price he had paid, Franz was not bitter. He was happy that his friend Albrecht had attained success.

One day Albrecht saw his loyal friend kneeling, his rough hands entwined in silent prayer. Albrecht quickly sketched the hands, later using the rough sketch to create his masterpiece known as "The Praying Hands."

10

Seasonal and Christian Year

A New Year's Prayer for Those Growing Older

Lord, thou knowest better than I know myself that I am growing older and will someday be old. Keep me from the fatal habit of thinking I must say something on every subject and on every occasion. Release me from craving to try to straighten out everybody's affairs.

Make me thoughtful but not moody; helpful but not bossy. With my vast store of wisdom, it seems a pity not to use it all—but thou knowest Lord, that I want a few friends at the end.

Keep my mind from the recital of endless details—give me wings to get to the point. Seal my lips on my aches and pains. They are increasing and the love of rehearsing them is becoming sweeter as the years go by.

I dare not ask for grace enough to enjoy the tales of others, but help me to endure them with patience.

Teach me to be reasonably sweet. I don't want to be a saint—some of them are so hard to live with—but a sour old person is one of the crowning works of the devil.

Give me the ability to see good things in unexpected places and talents in unexpected people. Give me the grace to tell them so. Through Jesus Christ our Lord. Amen.

A Gift for the New Year

As long as mortals have the nerve
To pray for things they don't deserve;
As long as conscience has a stain,
The prayers of men will be in vain.

So, humbly, Lord, we ask of thee
that princely gift, sincerity,
That we may use it through life's span
To build on earth a better man.
And should we crave for gifts more royal,
Please make us, God, a bit more loyal,

That we may give to those we serve
A measure full as they deserve.

And make us rich with eager zest
To give our work our very best;
To know the wheat, reject the chaff—
To have the strength to stand the gaff.

O Lord, in mercy intervene
To keep our hearts both young and clean,
The will to give a man a lift—
Make this, O Lord, thy New Year gift.

—Author unknown

The God Who Knows

I do not know the future,
    But I know the God who
    knows,
And in his perfect wisdom,
    Unknowing, I repose.

What good could come of
    knowing?
    How little I could do
To meet the joys or sorrows
    That I am coming to!

I do not know the future,
    But I know the God who
    knows,
I make his love my study
    And follow where he
    goes.

The path, its joys and sor-
    rows,
    I do not care to trace;
Content to know his good-
    ness,
    His mercy, and his grace.
                —William Luff

The Victorious Jesus

They cut the branches from
    the trees
    And strewed them in the
    way,
Because they knew their
    Lord and King
    Would come along that
    way.

They sang hosanna to the
    King
    And praised His holy
    name—
Now even in this modern
    day,
    We, too, should do the
    same.

The Christ who came that
    palm-strewn way
    To enter in the gate,
Will enter in your heart to-
    day,
    So do not make Him wait.

That palm-strewn path of
    long ago
    Is still a victory sign
That Christ still comes
    along the way
    Into your heart and mine.
                —Raymond Orner

A Mother's Beatitudes

Blessed is the mother who understands her child, for she shall inherit a kingdom of memories.

Blessed is the mother who knows how to comfort, for she shall possess a child's devotion.

Blessed is the mother who guides by the path of righteousness, for she shall be proud of her children.

Blessed is the mother who is never shocked, for she shall receive and know confidence and security.

Blessed is the mother who teaches respect, for she shall be respected.

Blessed is the mother who emphasizes the good and minimizes the bad, for her children shall follow her example.

Blessed is the mother who answers questions honestly, for she shall always be trusted.

Blessed is the mother who treats her children as she would like to be treated, for her home shall always be filled with happiness.

A Prayer for Mother's Day

Lord Jesus, you have known a mother's love and tender care; and you will hear, while for our own mothers most dear, we offer this Mother's Day prayer. Protect the lives, we pray, of those who have given us the gift of life. May our mothers know from day to day the deepening glow of joy that comes from your presence. We cannot pay our debts for all the love that we have received; but you, Lord, will not forget their due reward. Bless our mothers both in earth and heaven. Through Jesus Christ our Lord. Amen.

—Henry Van Dyke

Just Like His Dad

"Well, what are you going to be,
  my boy
  When you have reached man-
  hood's years:
A doctor, a lawyer, or actor great,
  Moving throngs to laughter and
  tears?"

But he shook his head, as he
  gave reply
  In the serious way he had:
"I don't think I'd care to be any of
  them:
  I want to be like my dad."

He wants to be like his dad! You
  men,
  Did you ever think, as you
  pause,
That the boy who watches your
  every move
  Is building a set of laws?

He's molding a life you're the
  model for,
And whether it's good or bad
Depends on the kind of example
  set
  To the boy who'd be like his
  dad.

Would you have him go everywhere you go?
  Have him do just the things you
  do?
And see everything that your
  eyes behold,
  And woo all the gods you woo?

When you see the worship that
  shines in the eyes
  Of your lovable little lad,
Could you rest content if he gets
  his wish
  And grows up to be like his
  dad?

—Author unknown

Memorial Day

From out our crowded cal-
   endar
One day we pluck to give;
It is the day the dying pause
To honor those who live.
   —McLandburgh Wilson

A Prayer for Independence Day

God of our fathers, whose almighty hand has made and preserved our nation, grant that our people may understand what it is they celebrate on Independence Day.

May they remember how bitterly our freedom was won, the down payment that was made for it, the installments that have been made since the Republic was born, and the price that must yet be paid for our liberty.

May we think of freedom not as the right to do as we please, but as the opportunity to please to do what is right.

May it ever be understood that our liberty is under God and can be found nowhere else.

May our faith be something that is not merely stamped upon our coins, but expressed in our lives.

To the extent that America honors thee, wilt thou bless America. Keep her true as thou hast kept her free, and make her good as thou hast made her rich. Through Jesus Christ our Lord. Amen.

—Peter Marshall

Our Flag

The flag is the emblem of our unity, our power, our thought and purpose as a nation. It has no other character than that which we give it from generation to generation.

The choices are ours. It floats in majestic silence above the hosts that execute these choices, whether in peace or war. And yet, though silent, it speaks to us—speaks to us of the past, of the men and women who went before us, and of the records they wrote upon it.

—Woodrow Wilson

Counting Our Blessings

O precious Father, as we bow
Before thy throne to-day—
We count the many blessings
Thou hast shower'd upon our way.

The comfort of our humble homes,
Our health and happiness,
The strength provided for each day
To meet the strain and stress.

We thank thee for thy precious Son
Who brought salvation free,
And for this mighty land of ours—
A land of liberty!

So, Lord, help us to give thee thanks
For all that we hold dear—
Not only on Thanksgiving Day
But each day of the year!
—Author unknown

A Thanksgiving Prayer

We thank thee, God, for blessings—
The big ones and the small—
Thy tender love and mercy
That guards and keeps us all.

The fresh awakening of joy
That comes with morning light,
Sunlit hours to fill the day
And restful sleep at night.

The hope, the beauty, and the love
That brighten each day's living—
We praise thee, and our hearts are filled
With joy, and with thanksgiving.

The pride that's found in work well done,
The love of those who care,
The peace of mind, the sweet content
That comes with quiet prayer.
—Author unknown

God's Christmas Gift

The tag: "For unto you is born this day in the city of David a Saviour, which is Christ the Lord" (Luke 2:11).

The wrapping: "And this shall be a sign unto you; ye shall find the babe wrapped in swaddling clothes, lying in a manger" (Luke 2:12).

The trimmings: "And suddenly there was with the angel a multitude of the heavenly host praising God, and saying, "Glory to God in the highest, and on earth peace, good will toward men" (Luke 2:13, 14).

The contents: "But when the fulness of the time was come, God sent forth his Son, made of a woman, made under the law, to redeem them that were under the law, that we might receive the adoption of sons" (Gal. 4:4, 5).

More Than Gifts

May Christmas time mean more
    to you
  Than gifts on Christmas morn;
May you feel the peace the whole
    world knew
  When Christ the Lord was
  born!

May you know the special glad-
    ness
  And hope that came to men;
And may it thrill your heart just
    now
  As Christmas comes again!
        —Author unknown

A Sweet Christmas

Why shouldn't this Christmas be
 sweeter
Than ever a Christmas before,
When Jesus is tenfold the dearer,
Outpouring His grace more and
 more?

Why shouldn't the future be
 brighter
With glad expectations each
 day?
Why shouldn't each burden
 seem lighter
With Jesus our King on the way?

Why shouldn't our vision be
 clearer,
His last blest command to obey,
While ever His coming draws
 nearer,
And millions in darkness still
 stray?

Oh, thus can this Christmas be
 sweeter
Than ever a Christmas before,
If souls that are dying are dearer,
And on them Christ's love we out-
 pour.
—Alice R. Flower

The True Spirit of Christmas

"What is Christmas?"
I asked my soul,
And this answer
Came back to me:
"It is the
Glory of heaven come
     down
In the hearts of humanity—
Come in the spirit and heart
     of a Child,
And it matters not what we
     share
At Christmas; it is not
     Christmas at all
Unless the Christ Child be
     there."
          —Author unknown